GW00913388

Halogen Cooking Made Easy...

Paul Brodel & Dee Hunwicks

Why We Love Halogen Cooking

What is Halogen ?...
Halogen is the gas used around the filament in the bulb.

Before electricity in the home, kitchens generally had a large fired oven and / or an open fire with a hand cranked spit (rotisserie)
The spit was used for cooking things like whole lamb, suckling pig, chickens and other poultry and fowl.

The intense radiant heat seared and sealed the meat on the outside, keeping it succulent and juicy on the inside.
This method of cooking renders down the natural fat of the meat which drips from it leaving it, lower in fat. No additional fat being required.

In a conventional oven fat is generally added to the cooking so the meat doesn't dry out or stick to the baking dish resulting in less healthy food.

The Halogen Oven is a modern day method of achieving similar results to spit and open fire roasting effortlessly, and tastes amazing.

Halogen Oven Cooking Accessories
(available with some models)

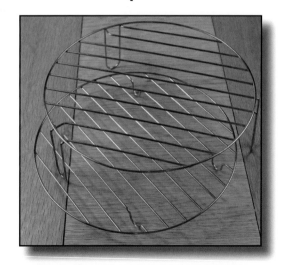

High Rack & Low Rack

Low Rack - used for roasting.
High Rack - used for grilling.

Round Halogen Oven Tray

Steamer Rack / Diffuser

Tongs

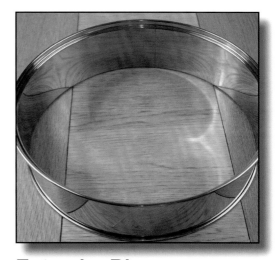

Extender Ring
Used to raise the lid and slow down the cooking process.

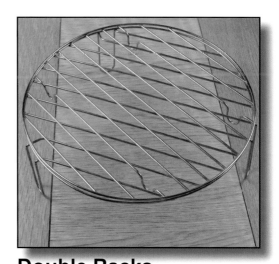

Double Racks
Low rack on top of the high rack crossed to prevent smaller foods dropping though when grilling.

Clean with hot soapy water or place in the dishwasher.
The bowl can also be used independently for other things, i.e. salad bowl, punch bowl.

Glass Halogen Bowl

Getting Started with your Halogen Oven

The Halogen Oven is an excellent tool to have in your kitchen, and is brilliant for cooking a diverse range of foods which means the possibilities are endless. This book aims to guide you along your way, giving you recipes which we hope will give you confidence and pleasure in using your Halogen Oven. Please remember this is a rough guide and ensure that all food is cooked thoroughly before serving.

Some models do not go up to 250°c. In that case please put up to the highest temperature and adjust the cooking time accordingly until thoroughly cooked.

Low Rack - used for roasting *High Rack* - used for grilling

Extender Ring - used to raise the lid, give an even heat and slow down the cooking process. Particularly good for foods you don't want to grill but need to cook with an even heat.

Cookware - We use a variety of dishes, tin and glass oven dishes (that can also be used under a grill) when cooking in the Halogen Oven. (You can use Silicon bake ware, however I do advise that you only use in temperatures up to 180 degrees and only on the lower rack with the extender ring to avoid burning).

Grilling on the High Rack - Rough guide
Chops - 6-8 minutes each side -
Chicken breasts - 8-10 minutes each side
Bacon - 3-5 minutes each side -
Burgers - 6-10 minutes each side
Steaks – Rare 2-5 minutes each side - Medium 5-7 minutes each side - Well done 7-10 minutes on each side.
(Remember the amount of time also depends on the thickness of the chosen food). If using pre-prepared frozen foods always follow manufacturers instructions.

Roasting Vegetables - Root Vegetables
Place on a tray with oil on the low rack - Temp 240°c - Time 30 minutes (turning every 7 or until cooked).

Cooking Meat

When cooking meat joints it's best to opt for larger, thinner pieces of meat as these cook faster than compact meat joints (which tend to take longer to cook through to the centre).

Chicken Small 2-3lb/ Medium 3-4½lb - Cook on low rack and turn every 10-15 minutes to ensure even and thorough cooking. Cook at 220 degrees for 45 minutes* then 180 degrees for a further 45 minutes, for a medium sized chicken cook for a further 10 minutes or until juices run clear after piercing with a knife.

Lamb Joint - 3lb/1½kg - Cook on a low rack - Cook at 240 degrees for 10 minutes, turn and cook for further 10 minutes* then cook at 180 degrees for 60 minutes, turn every 15 minutes and cook for further 30 minutes if required well done.

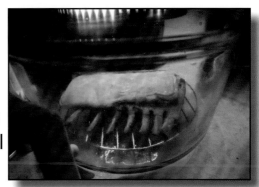

Pork joint - 2lb/1kg (rub with salt prior to cooking) - Cook on a low rack at 220 degrees for 60 minutes, turn every 15 minutes* then cook at 180 degrees for further 30 minutes. Check juices run clear by piercing with a knife - continue cooking till juices run clear.

Beef Joint - 2lb/1kg - Cook on low rack at 240 degrees for 30 minutes, turn every 10 minutes* then cook at 180 degrees for 10 minutes = rare/blue, 30 minutes = medium or 50 minutes = well done.

* you can add your par boiled potatoes and vegetables to the Halogen Oven for roasting at this point.

Top tips for your halogen oven...

1) When steaming vegetables always use boiling water in the base of your oven to save time on heating up. Place the boiling water in first before turning the cooker on. I tend to put vegetables on the low rack. The high rack is placed on top with the round oven tray filled with boiling

water which will generate the steam. When the halogen oven is turned on, the steam created by the water is moved around the cooker by the fan. I steam at 250°c.
Only suitable for things that are very quick to steam. (The steam is so hot it vaporized so invisible). You can wrap vegetables in tin foil, with a little water and cook them whilst roast-ing with your meats, time depending on vegetables & thickness.

2) When grilling such things as bacon you can put tin foil in the base, or a cup full of water to the base of the halogen oven bowl, then any dripping fat floats on the top of the water and doesn't stick to the bowl, making it easier top clean. If you cook meats that spit, cook on the low rack to grill.

3) As a rough guide when cooking meat joints on the low rack, I tend to

start on a high heat to seal the meat. This keeps the juices in. Then lower to the temperature required. When cooking things that you want well done, I use the extender ring to make the cooking process more   gen-tle. This will cook the meat more evenly. I also tend to turn joints during cooking.

4) When cooking casseroles, always use an oven dish that fits in the halogen bowl so air can circulate round. In this dish, cook off the meat first with the vegetables in the Halogen oven at 250°c. Then I add the liquid and cover with foil wrap. I have also used oven proof glass lids to keep the liquid in and stop it from drying out. I then turn down the temperature as for a regular oven.

When referring to measurements
As a very rough guide :

tsp = teaspoon
(heaped slightly unless it's liquid) 5ml
one teaspoon = ½ dessert spoon
dsp = dessert spoon
(normally heaped slightly unless it's a liquid)
one dessert spoon = ½ a tablespoon

tbsp normally = tablespoon
(heaped slightly unless it's a liquid)
one tablespoon = two dessert spoons

25g or 1oz is 1 tablespoon of flour (heaped).
25g or 1 oz is 1 tablespoon of sugar (not so heaped).

25g = 1oz
50g = 2 oz
75g = 3 oz
100g = 4 oz
450g = 16 oz = 1lb

All temperatures given are a rough guide, always check the food has been thoroughly cooked before consumption, especially poultry and pork. Always refer to manufactures instructions as models may vary.

150ml = ¼ pint = 5fl oz
300ml = ½ pint = 10fl oz
600ml = 1 pint = 20fl oz
1.1litres = 2 pints = 40fl oz

1cm = ½ inch
2.5cm = 1inch
15cm = 6 inches

If you are using a "Rotisserie Halogen Oven" and the maximum heat setting is lower than the recipe states, adjust the cooking time accordingly until thoroughly cooked.

CONTENTS / INDEX

Starters:

Main Courses:

Main Courses: (Continued)

Desserts:

Cheats Sushi

Ingredients
200g sushi rice
240g boiling water
½ tbsp Mirin rice wine
½ tbsp Japanese rice vinegar
6 large cooked prawns (deveined & halved)
2 sheet nori leaf
½ avocado slice in strips
6 fish sticks
100g smoked salmon
Brush ingredients
1 tbsp Mirin wine vinegar
1 tbsp Japanese rice vinegar
1 tbsp water
Makes roughly 33 pieces

Method
1. Rinse the rice by placing in a bowl and stirring with cold water running through it, then drain.
2. Place back in a bowl and pour over boiling water and drain, repeat this three times. Then add in an oven proof dish the hot drained rice and measured amount of boiling water and cover with tin foil.
3. Pour a cup of boiling water in the base of the halogen oven then place the rice on the low rack & cook for 20 minutes at 250°C, after this time leave the bowl of rice in the halogen oven for 20 minutes with no heat.
4. Remove the rice from the oven (the rice should be sticky) and add ½ tbsp Mirin wine vinegar & ½ tbsp Japanese rice vinegar & mix.
5. Mix the brush ingredients together & brush a silicon sheet, place the rice on the sheet shape and roll into an oblong.
6. Cut into shape and make, smoked salmon sushi, prawn sushi & Nori rolls (brush Nori leaf with brush mix to make it stick, fill with fish stick, rice and avocado and roll. as per pictures.
Serve with wasabi, soy sauce and pickled ginger.

13

Chicken Soup

Ingredients

2 chicken breasts
1 onion (chopped)
1 tsp garlic puree
1 tbsp arrowroot
2 tbsp double cream
300ml milk
200ml chicken stock
200ml boiling water
½ tbsp olive oil
Salt & pepper
Garnish
Fresh parsley (chopped)
Serve with crusty bread
Serves 2-4

Method

1. Add the chicken, onions, garlic puree, & oil to a large heat proof bowl. Cook on the low rack at 250°c for 10 minutes.
2. Add the cream, chicken stock and season well. Cook for 10 minutes.
3. Mix the arrowroot with a little water, add to the soup & cook for 5 minutes.
4. Stir in the milk with 200ml of boiling water & blend (this makes a thick soup add more milk if you prefer a thinner soup).
Add a teaspoon of curry powder at method 1, for a chicken curry soup.

15

Chilli Chicken Wings

Ingredients
475g chicken wings
1 tsp tomato paste
2 tbsp sweet chilli sauce
1 tsp ginger paste
1 tsp garlic paste
1 tbsp mayonnaise
Garnish
Lime wedges
Serve with salad.
Serves 4

Method

1. Mix the tomato paste, sweet chilli sauce; ginger, garlic & mayonnaise, in a large bowl. Add the chicken & coat with the sauce.
2. Pour the mixture onto the round tray & cook on the high rack at 250°c for 10 minutes stirring every 2-3 minutes.
3. Turn the temperature down to 200°c. Stir & cook for 5 minutes, stirring halve way through the cooking time.
   Great on a picnic.

Curried Parsnip Soup

Ingredients

4 Parsnips (small dice)
1 Onion (chopped)
1 tbsp Curry powder
2 Bay leaves
½ tsp Mixed herbs
2 tbsp Vegetable or chicken stock
550m warm milk
25g Butter
Salt & pepper
Garnish
Parsley
Serve with mini popadoms.
Serves 2-4

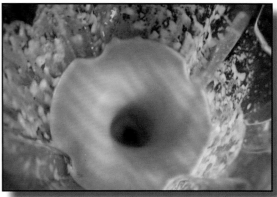

Method

1. Chop the parsnips into a small dice (this stops the soup being stringy).
2. Add parsnips, curry powder, onions, mixed herbs, bay leafs & butter to a large heatproof bowl. Place on the low rack at 250°c for 10 minutes.
3. Add the stock, stir & cook for a further 15 minutes.
4. Pour the soup into a blender add the warm milk, season & blend. (add more milk if you prefer a thinner soup).
   Can be served with naan bread.

Devils on Horseback

Ingredients
1 Cup black tea
12 Prunes
12 rashers streaky bacon
12 Toothpicks
50g orange marmalade
½ chicken stock cube
(mixed with 50ml boiling water)
Pinch of black pepper
Serve with crusty bread.
Serves 2

Method
1. Soak the prunes in the black tea for 30 minutes.
2. Drain and roll the prunes in the bacon & skewer with the toothpicks.
3. Place on the round tray on the high rack at 250°c & cook for 5 minutes on each side.
4. Drain off excess fat & dry with a paper towel
5. Mix together the stock & marmalade & together pour over the prunes & cook for 2 minutes on each side.
6. Season with black pepper & serve.
   Great as a party dish.

21

Green Lipped Mussels with a Cheese & Chilli Topping

Ingredients

16 frozen pre-cooked
        Green lipped mussels
100g Cheddar cheese (grated)
3 tbsp sweet chilli sauce
Pinch ground pepper
Garnish
Parsley & lemon
Serve with crusty bread & salad.
Serves 4

Method

1. Place your open mussels, shell side down, onto the round tin.
2. Mix together the grated cheese, sweet chilli sauce & pepper. Spoon equal amounts of the mixture on top of each mussel & cook on the high rack for 10 minutes or until golden brown, at 250°c.
   Can grill the mussels with garlic butter instead.

Stuffed Mushrooms

Ingredients
5 Portabella mushrooms
50g emmental cheese (grated)
150g cream cheese with garlic & herbs
5 slices Chorizo
Salt & pepper
Serve with salad & crusty bread.
Serves 5

Method

1. Place a slice of Chorizo on each mushroom & put on the round tray. Cook on the high rack at 250°c for 2 minutes.
2. Stuff each mushroom with cream cheese & sprinkle with the emmental cheese / cheese of you choice. Cook on the low rack at 250°c for 8 minutes or until golden brown.
   Leave out the Chorizo for a vegetarian starter.

Tuna Potato Melt

Ingredients
1 tin of tuna in brine (drained)
4 medium sized baking potatoes
2oz cheddar cheese - grated
1 onion finely chopped
1 tsp tomato ketchup
2 tbsp mayonnaise
Salt & pepper
Garnish
Parsley sprig
Serve with a mixed salad.
Serves 4

Method
1. Wash & dry the potatoes & place them on the low rack at 250°c turning every 15 minutes. Cook for 45 minutes - 1 hour or until cooked.
2. When cooked, remove potatoes & slice in half length ways.
   Partially scoop out the cooked potato & mix in a bowl with the tuna, mayonnaise, onion & tomato ketchup.
3. Fill the potato skins with the mixture. & Sprinkle with grated cheddar cheese.
4. Cook the potato on the high rack at 250°c for 5 minutes or until golden brown.

Tinned ham or salmon works well instead of tuna.

27

Beef Wellington

Ingredients

1 200g sheet ready rolled puff pastry
1 mushroom (finely chopped)
¼ white onion (finely chopped)
1 tsp brown fruity sauce
10g butter (cubed)
2 100g beef fillet steaks
1 egg (to glaze)
Salt and pepper
***Serve with roast potatoes
and vegetables.***
Serves 2

Method

1. Unroll the pastry and cut into 4 squares. Place 2 of the squares on the greased round tray and cook on the low rack at 250°c for 2 minutes.
2. Mix the mushroom, onion and fruity sauce together in a bowl. Spoon the mixture equally between the pastry squares and spread evenly. Add a piece of butter on top of each. Cook on the low rack at 250°c for 3 minutes.
3. Season the beef well with salt and pepper. Place each piece of meat onto the pastry squares and cook on the low rack at 250°c for 2 minutes. Turn the beef over and cook for a further 2 minutes.(for rare meat just add the pastry top).
4. Add the other 2 pastry squares on top of the beef and glaze with egg. Cook on the low rack at 160°c for 15 minutes or until cooked.
Can use home made burgers instead of fillet steak and sweet pickle instead of mushrooms, onions and fruity sauce.

29

Beef with Black Bean Sauce

Ingredients
250g rump steak (thinly sliced)
½ red pepper (sliced)
½ yellow pepper (sliced)
4 broccoli florets (thinly sliced)
10 cherry tomatoes (halved)
50g mushrooms (sliced)
½ white onion (sliced)
220g jar black bean sauce
1 tsp sesame oil
1 garlic clove (finely chopped)
Serve with rice.
Serves 4

Method

1. Put the rump steak, red pepper, yellow pepper, broccoli slices, cherry tomatoes, mushrooms, onion, sesame oil and garlic in a large heat proof dish that will fit in the Halogen oven. Mix well.
2. Place the dish on the low rack at 250°c for 10 minutes, stirring every 5 minutes.
3. Add the black bean sauce & cook for 15 minutes stirring every 5 minutes or until cooked.
   Can use chicken or prawns instead vary times accordingly.

Burgers

Ingredients
500g minced beef
1 onion finely chopped
1 tbsp ploughmans sweet pickle
1 tsp garlic granuals
Serve in a bun with chips, salad & relish.
Serves 6

Method
1. Chop the sweet pickle on a chopping board to a fine consistency (like you would chop parsley on a board).
2. Mix all the ingredients together in a bowl.
3. Form into burgers, about 6.
4. Grill on high rack on round tray at 250°c for 6 minute on each side or until cooked.
   These burgers are so tasty.
   To make them extra special melt blue cheese on the top or serve with bacon or avocado.

33

Chicken Curry

Ingredients
400g chicken breast (diced)
13g butter
1 white onion (diced)
½ tbsp curry powder
1 tsp garlic paste
1 tsp ginger paste
½ chicken stock cube
(mixed with 200ml boiling water)
4 dried apricots (chopped)
1 tsp flour
50g frozen peas
1 tbsp soy sauce
75 fl oz double cream
Pepper to season
Serve with rice and poppadums.
Serves 2-3

Method

1. Put the chicken breast, butter, onion, curry powder, garlic paste and ginger paste in a large heat proof oven dish. Mix well. Cook on the low rack at 250°c for 10 minutes, stirring after 5 minutes.
2. Stir again. Add the flour & mix then add chicken stock, apricots, frozen peas and soy sauce. Continue to cook on the low rack at 250°c for 15 minutes.
3. Add the double cream, season well with pepper and stir. Cook for a further 5 minutes or until cooked.
   Works well with a meat substitute or mushrooms instead of chicken.

Chicken Fajita Wraps

Ingredients

2 chicken breasts (cut into strips)
½ onion (sliced)
½ red pepper (sliced)
50g mushrooms (halved)
1 tsp chilli powder
½ tsp garlic salt
1 tsp ground cumin
½ chicken stock cube
(mixed with 25ml boiling water)
***Serve with wraps, sour cream, salsa
and grated cheese.***
Serves 4

Method

1. Put the chicken, onion, red pepper, mushrooms, chilli powder, garlic salt, ground cumin and stock cube in a large bowl. Stir well.
2. Put the mixture on the round tray and cook on the low rack at 250°c for 7 minutes. Turn with tongs and cook for a further 10 minutes or until cooked.
   Make home made avocado dip with soft avocado mixed with sweet chilli sauce and mayonnaise.

Cod in Parma Ham with Parsley Butter

Ingredients
Fillet of cod (240g) sliced lengthways
25g butter
2 slices parma ham
Sprig of parsley (chopped)
Salt and pepper to season
Serve with new potatoes and vegetables.
Serves 2

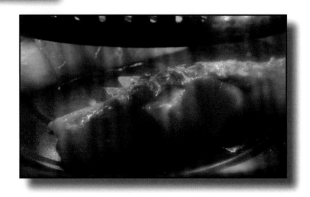

Method

1. Lay the slices of parma ham on the round tray. Place a cod fillet width ways on top of each.
2. Mix the butter and parsley in a small bowl.
3. Divide the butter mixture into quarters and place one piece on top of each fillet. Bring up the sides of the ham underneath each fillet to wrap. Place another piece of butter on top of each.
4. Put the round tray onto the high rack and cook at 250°c for 5 minutes. Turn down to 200°c & cook for a further 10 minutes or until cooked. **Try using monkfish instead of cod.**

Cod with a Tomato & Caper Dressing

Ingredients
2 fillet cod
½ lemon (juiced)
1 tomato (diced)
½ tbsp capers
1 tbsp oil
3 sprigs parsley (chopped)
2 spring onions (sliced)
Salt & pepper
Garnish
½ fresh lemon
Serve with new potatoes & salad.
Serves 2

Method

1. Rub the cod fillets with oil & place on the round tray. Cook on the high rack at 250°c for 8 minutes.
2. Combine the diced tomato, spring onions, parsley & lemon juice. Place on top of the cod fillets & cook on the high rack at 250°c for 2 minutes or until cooked.
   Try using halibut instead of cod.

41

Duck and Hoisin Wraps

Ingredients
1 duck breast (thinly sliced)
4 spring onions (sliced length ways)
½ red pepper (sliced)
½ yellow pepper (sliced)
50g mushrooms (sliced)
2 tbsp plum sauce
1 tbsp hoisin sauce
½ tsp garlic paste
¼ tsp ginger paste
½ tsp sesame oil
1 tsp soy sauce
Serve with tortilla wraps.
Serves 4

Method

1. Put the duck breast, spring onions, red pepper, yellow pepper, mushrooms, plum sauce, hoisin sauce, garlic paste, ginger paste, sesame oil and soy sauce in a large mixing bowl. Stir so that all the ingredients are well mixed.
2. Place all the ingredients onto the round tray and cook on the low rack at 250°c for 17 – 20 minutes or until cooked, stirring after 10 minutes
Try using chicken instead of duck and adjust time accordingly.

Eastern Mint Ribs

Ingredients
550g lamb ribs
1 tsp ginger paste
1 tsp garlic paste
1 tsp ground cumin
1 tbsp mint jelly
1 sprig rosemary (chopped)
1 tbsp yoghurt
Serve with cous cous & sultanas.
Serves 4-6

Method

1. In a pan on your conventional hob boil the lamb ribs for 45 minutes. This will help take some of the greasiness away.
2. While the lamb is cooking put the yoghurt, ginger paste, & garlic paste, ground cumin, mint jelly & rosemary together in a bowl. Mix well.
3. When the ribs are cooked, drain & dry on kitchen paper.
4. Pour the yoghurt mixture over the cooked ribs, turning them so they are thoroughly coated. Place on the round baking tray on the high rack at 250°c for approximately 12 minutes until starting to brown.
   Can use cranberry or red currant jelly instead of mint jelly.

Gammon Steaks with a Cheesy Bread Crumb Topping

Ingredients
2 gammon steaks
50g breadcrumbs
50g cheddar cheese (grated)
1 sprig of parsley (chopped)
Pinch salt & pepper to season
1 tsp mustard
1 tbsp runny honey
Garnish
Sprig of parsley
Serve with new potatoes and beans.
Serves 2

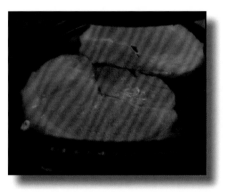

Method

1. Cook the gammon steaks on the round tray, on the low rack at 250°c for 10 minutes.
2. Mix the bread crumbs, parsley, cheese, salt & pepper. Mix the honey & mustard in a separate bowl.
3. After 10 minutes cooking, turn the gammon steaks over & coat with the honey & mustard mixture. Spread the breadcrumb mixture on top, avoiding the rind of the gammon so it becomes crispy. Cook on the low rack at 250°c for 5 minutes. Then turn down to 200°c and cook for a further 5 minutes.

Can use a flattened chicken breast instead of gammon.

47

Kidneys in a Mushroom & Bacon Sauce

Ingredients

5 kidneys (sliced) (white core removed)
2 rashers Back bacon (sliced)
1 onion (sliced)
5 mushrooms (halved)
1 tbsp olive oil
250ml beef gravy (made up granules)
1 beef stock cube
Flour to coat
Serve with mash & peas.
Serves 3

Method

1. Mix the kidneys, bacon, onions & mushrooms with the flour. Coat the round tray with the olive oil & place on the top rack cook for 5 minutes at 250°c.
2. Turn the kidneys, bacon over & cook for a further 5 minutes.
3. Add the gravy & sprinkle with the stock cube. Stir & cook for a further 10 minutes.
   Works well with chopped chicken livers adjust times accordingly.

Lamb Chops with a Parmesan & Mustard Crust

Ingredients
5 lamb cutlets
40g freshly grated parmesan
2 tbsp runney honey
1 heaped tsp English mustard
50g white bread crumbs
1 tsp mixed dried herbs
pinch salt & pepper
Serve with mashed potatoes, carrots & gravy
Serves 2

Method

1. Place the lamb cutlets on the round baking tray & cook on the high rack for 3 minutes each side. Remove, dry on a paper towel and set aside.
2. Mix together the honey & the mustard in a bowl coat each lamb cutlet on both sides.
3. In a separate bowl combine the breadcrumbs, mixed dried herbs, salt & pepper & parmesan cheese. Roll each lamb cutlet into the bread crumb mixture until evenly coated.
4. Place on a greased round baking tray & cook on the high rack at 250c for 5 minutes each side or until cooked.
Works well with a rack of lamb instead.

Lemon & Herb Chicken

Ingredients
6 chicken thighs (skinned & boned)
1 lemon (juiced)
1 tsp mixed herbs
1 tsp garlic puree
½ tbsp olive oil
Pinch salt & pepper
Garnish
Salad
Serve with sweet mash potato.
Serves 3

Method

1. Mix juice of lemon, herbs, garlic puree, salt, pepper & olive oil together. Coat chicken with mixture & place on the round tray, on the high rack at 250°c. Cook for 15 minutes, turning every 5 minutes.
2. Make sure the chicken is piping hot & cooked all the way through.
   Works well with white fish instead of chicken.

53

Lemon Sole Stuffed with Prawns

Ingredients
2 fillets lemon sole (185g each fillet)
125g ready to eat prawns
25g butter (room temperature)
1 clove garlic (finely chopped)
1 sprig parsley (finely chopped)
1 lemon
Salt & pepper
Cooks string to secure
Serve with new potatoes and mange tout.
Serves 2

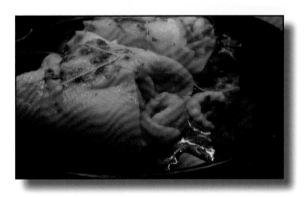

Method

1. Make the garlic butter by mixing the garlic, parsley & butter in a bowl. Divide into four.
2. Take your lemon sole fillets & spoon half the prawns on top of each fillet. Add a piece of the garlic butter, squeeze of lemon & roll up the fillet, season with salt & pepper, secure with a piece of cooks string. Add another piece of the garlic butter on top.
3. Place the fillets on the round tray & cook on the low rack at 200°c for 20 minutes or until cooked.

Meatballs in a Creamy Mushroom Sauce

Ingredients

Meatballs
300g minced beef
1 tbsp plain flour
½ tsp garlic salt
¼ tsp mixed herbs

Sauce
1 onion (sliced)
5 mushrooms (sliced)
1 clove garlic (chopped)
1 tsp plain flour
1 tsp mustard
100ml double cream
100ml milk
1 dsp ketjap Manis - thick sweet indonesian soy sauce or use dark soy sauce

Garnish
Fresh Parsley
Serve with steamed rice or new potatoes & lingonberry or cranberry sauce.
Serves 4-6

Method

1. Combine the minced beef, 1 tbsp flour, garlic salt & mixed herbs together roll in to small meatballs. (Makes approximately 15)
2. Place the meatballs & onions on the round tray on the high rack at 250°c for 5 minutes.
3. Stir in the mushrooms & garlic. Cook for 5 minutes then add the flour & mix.
4. Mix the cream, milk, mustard, ketjap manis in a bowl and stir into the meatballs. Turn down too 200°c & cook for 10 minutes, stirring every 2-3 minutes.

Use chicken strips instead of meat balls.

Mediterranean Lamb Kebabs

Ingredients
326g lamb (diced)
1 tsp dried mixed herbs
1 tsp garlic puree
½ chicken stock cube
½ lemon
1 white onion (quartered & separated)
1 yellow pepper (diced in large chunks)
1tsp olive oil
6 wooden kebab skewers
        (soaked in boiling water)
Serve with pitta bread, salad & a spoonful of soured cream mixed with mint jelly.
Serves 3

Method

1. Mix the chicken stock cube with a teaspoon of boiling water in a bowl. Add the garlic puree, dried mixed herbs, olive oil & half of the juice of the lemon.
2. Thread alternative pieces of lamb, onion & pepper on a skewer. Repeat until you have made 6 skewers.
3. Place the skewers on a flat dish & pour over the marinade. Use a Chefs brush to evenly coat the kebabs with the mixture.
4. Place the kebabs onto the round tray & cook on the high rack at 250°c for 5 minutes. Turn the kebabs & cook for a further 5 minutes. Turn again, reduce the temperature to 200°c. Cook for 5 minutes or until cooked.

Minced Beef Pie

Ingredients
500g minced beef
1 medium potato (peeled and diced)
1 carrot (peeled and diced)
2 onions (chopped)
1 tsp yeast extract
Salt and pepper
2 tsp plain flour
1 tbsp sweet pickle e.g. ploughman's
1 beef stock cube
4 heaped tsp gravy granules
280 ml boiling water
213g ready rolled puff pastry
½ tbsp milk to glaze
Serve with mashed potatoes and peas.
Serves 4

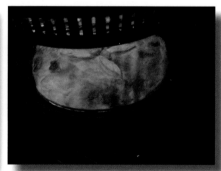

Method
1. Put the minced beef, potato, carrots, onions, salt and pepper in a large heat proof cooking bowl that will fit in Halogen oven. Mix well. Cook on the low rack at 250°c for 20 minutes stirring every 5 minutes
2. Place the gravy granules in a jug. Add the boiling water and stir.
3. Add the flour to the minced beef mixture & stir then add stock cube, sweet pickle, yeast extract, and gravy & stir.
4. Continue to cook on the low rack at 250°c for 5 minutes. Stir.
5. Take the ready rolled puff pastry and cut a lid to fit the top of the heat proof bowl. Add the lid on the top of the minced beef mixture.
6. Brush lightly with milk and cook on the low rack at 160°c for 20 minutes or until cooked.

Pizza

Ingredients
Dough
100ml warm milk (any type)
50ml warm water (not boiled)
1 tsp dried yeast
250g strong flour
2 tbsp olive oil
Pinch of salt
Filling
4 tbsp ketchup or tomato passata
25g cubed cheese
(feta, mozzarella or cheddar cheese)
25g cheddar cheese (grated)
50g salami
6 cherry tomatoes
6 basil leaves
Pinch mixed dried herbs
Serve with a mixed salad.
Serves 2 (cut in half)

Method
1. In a large bowl place the warm milk, water and dried yeast. Mix and leave for 5 minutes.
2. Add the flour and mix to form a dough. Kneed for 5 minutes or use a food mixer with a dough hook. Then kneed in the olive oil.
3. Cover the bowl with a damp tea towel and leave in a warm place to rise for 1 hour.
4. Add the salt to the dough and kneed into a large round circle to make the pizza base.
5. Pre heat the halogen oven at 250c for 2 minutes. Grease the base of the round tray and place the pizza base on top on the low rack. Cook at 250c for 5 minutes. Turn over and cook for further 5 minutes.
6. Spread the semi cooked base with the ketchup or passata, and then add the cubed cheese, salami, tomatoes, basil and mixed herbs. Sprinkle with the cheddar cheese.
7. Continue to cook for 10 minutes.

63

Pork Chops in Hoisin Sauce

Ingredients
4 pork loin steaks
Hoisin Glaze
1 tsp soy sauce
1 tsp brown sugar
1/2 tsp garlic salt
2 tbsp tomato sauce
2 tbsp Hoisin sauce
Serve with sweet potato & steamed broccoli.
Serves 4
(Instead of pork you can use lamb, chicken, beef or sausages)

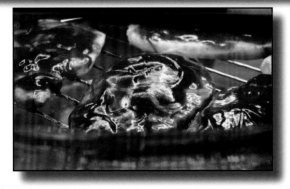

Method
1. Place the pork loin steaks on the round tray & cook on the high rack at 250°c for 10 minutes.
2. Make the sauce by combining the brown sugar, soy sauce, garlic salt, tomato sauce & hoisin sauce in a large bowl. Mix well.
3. After 10 minutes turn the pork loin steaks over. Generously apply the sauce over the top of the steaks (make sure they are well covered with a good coating of the sauce).
4. Cook for a further 5 minutes on the high rack at 250°c. Turn down to 200°c & cook for a further 5 minutes.
   Use the hoisin glaze on different meats.

Pork in a Orange & Marmalade Sauce

Ingredients

4 pork loin steaks
1 onion (finely chopped)
1 tbsp Arrowroot
¼ tsp mixed herbs
2 tbsp marmalade
1 tsp dark brown sugar
1 chicken stock cube
(with 100ml boiling water)
200ml orange juice
Serve with mash potatoes and peas.
Serves 4

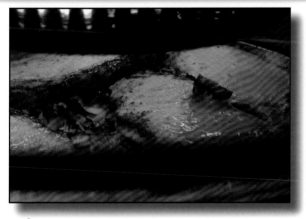

Method

1. Place the steaks & onions on to the round tray on the high rack at 250°c, cook for 7 minutes. Turn over the steaks & cook for a further 7 minutes.
2. Mix the arrowroot with a little orange juice in a oven proof dish to form a paste, then add the remaining orange juice, stock, marmalade, brown sugar & mixed herbs.
3. Put the pork & onions in the oven proof dish that fits in the Halogen oven & pour over the orange glaze.
4. Put the dish in the halogen oven on the low rack at 180°c for 35 minutes or until cooked.
Can use sausages instead of pork chops.

67

Pork Ribs In Sticky Sauce

Ingredients

350g Pork ribs
1 tbsp Tomato puree
2 tbsp fruity sauce
2 tbsp ketjap manis (sweet indonesian
    soy sauce or use dark soy sauce)
1 tbsp Honey
¼ tsp garlic salt
Serve with corn & mash potato.
Serves 4-6

Method

1. On a conventional hob top in a pan of boiling water, boil the pork ribs on the stove for 45 minutes.
2. When cooked, drain & dry on kitchen paper.
3. Mix together in a bowl, garlic salt, fruity sauce, ketjap Manis, honey & tomato puree in a bowl.
4. Coat the ribs thoroughly with the sticky marinade mixture & place on the round tray on the high rack at 250°c for 6 minutes on each side or until starting to brown.
   Can use a rack of ribs instead.

69

Pork Steaks in Pineapple Sauce

Ingredients
4 pork steaks
227g tin of cubed pineapple in juice
1 chicken stock cube
(mixed with 100ml boiling water)
1 onion (chopped)
1 tsp oil
1 tsp brown sugar
¼ tsp garlic salt
1 tbsp arrowroot
Salt & pepper
Serve with sweet mashed potato
& steamed courgettes.
Serves 4

Method

1. Rub pork steaks with garlic salt. Mix onions with oil & place on the round tray with pork steaks. Cook on the high rack at 250°c For 5 minutes on each side.
2. Place the arrowroot in a bowl & slowly stir in the pineapple juice. Add the pineapple, sugar & stock & mix.
3. Season the pork with salt & pepper & pour pineapple mix over the top. Cook on the low rack for 20 minutes or until cooked, stirring every 5 minutes.
Add 3 tbsp tomato sauce & 2 tsp of vinegar to the sauce for a sweet and sour sauce.

Quick Apricot Ginger & Garlic Lamb

Ingredients
350g diced lamb shoulder
1 tsp ground cumin
1 tsp ginger paste
1 tsp garlic paste
1 tbsp apricot jam
Salt & pepper
Serve in a pita bread with salad.
Serves 2-4

Method

1. Mix the ground cumin, ginger paste, garlic paste & apricot jam in a bowl.
2. Add the diced lamb & combine.
3. Put on the round tray & cook on the high rack at 250°c for 15 minutes, turning every 3 minutes.
   Great also served with cous cous.

Quiche Lorraine

Ingredients

Shortcrust pastry
200g plain flour
100g cold butter (cut into cubes)
Pinch of salt
A little cold water
Filling
50ml whole milk
25ml cream
2 - 4 eggs (depending on size of quiche dish)
100g cheddar cheese (grated)
5 rashers bacon (smoked is best) (chopped)
1 large onion (thinly sliced)
1 large tomato (sliced)
Salt and pepper   *Serves 4*

Method

1. To make the short crust pastry, put the flour, butter and salt into a food processor. Blitz until it looks like fine bread crumbs then add cold water, a little at a time until a dough is formed. (This will leave the sides of the mixing bowl clean).
2. Allow to rest in the fridge wrapped in cling film for 30 minutes.
3. Roll out the pastry and use to line a 22cm quiche dish. Prick the base of the pastry case with a fork. Cook on the low rack at 180°c for 20 minutes.
4. Whilst the pastry case is cooking, beat the eggs together in a bowl. After 20 minutes cooking time, remove the pastry case and glaze all over with a little of the beaten egg. Return to the halogen oven and cook on the low rack at 220°c for 7 minutes.
5. Add the onions and the bacon to the pasty case and cook on the low rack at 250c for 7 minutes.
6. 6) Add the beaten egg and the grated cheese (reserve a little cheese to sprinkling on the top) to the bacon and onion mixture. Add the sliced tomatoes on top and sprinkle with the remainder of the cheese and cook on the low rack at 175°c for 20 minutes. Turn down the temperature to 150°c and cook for a further 15 minutes or until cooked.

Sausages with Red Onion Gravy

Ingredients

8 sausages
2 red onions (sliced)
1 tbsp balsamic glaze
250 ml beef gravy
1 beef stock cube

Serve with potato & sweet potato mash & steamed vegetables.
Serves 4

Method

1. Place the sausages on the round tray. Add the red onion slices around the sausages. Cook on the high rack at 250°c for 5 minutes then turn the sausages. Cook for a further 5 minutes and turn. Cook for a further 4 minutes and turn the onions.
2. Add the balsamic glaze to the gravy mixture, together with the stock cube. Stir.
3. Turn the sausages over to show their lightest colouring then pour over the gravy mixture. Cook for a further 6 minutes.
   Can add sliced mushrooms to sauce at the same time you add the onions.

Spanish Style Cottage Pie

Ingredients
300g Minced beef
2 tsp plain flour
3 medium potatoes (cubed)
1 sweet potato (cubed)
1 onion (chopped)
50g chorizo
4 mushrooms (sliced)
1 carrot (peeled & sliced)
1 clove garlic (chopped)
400g chopped tomatoes
1 tbsp tomato puree
25g butter
1 beef stock cube in 100ml boiling water
Salt & pepper
Serve with steamed broccoli.
Serves 4-6

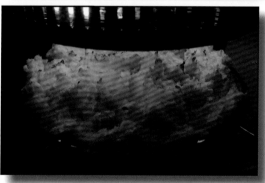

Method

1. Boil potatoes & sweet potatoes on a hob for 20 minutes to make the mash topping. Drain, mash & add butter, salt & pepper.
2. Place the beef, chorizo & onion in a 1 ¾ - 2 litre ovenproof dish.
3. Put on the low rack at 250°c for 6 minutes stirring after 3 minutes.
4. Add the carrots, garlic, tomato puree, & mushrooms, flour, stir & cook for 6 minutes.
5. Stir in the chopped tomatoes & beef stock. Cook for 20 minutes stirring every 5 minutes.
6. Put the mash topping on the cooked mince, turn down to 150°c. Cook for 12 minutes or until golden brown.
   Can add grated cheese on top of the mash.

Steak with Blue Cheese

Ingredients
1 thin cut Sirloin steak (110g)
1 onion (sliced)
1 tsp olive oil
¼ tsp garlic salt
¼ tsp ground black pepper
50g / 2 oz blue cheese
Garnish
Ground pepper & fresh parsley
Serve with mash potato & steamed broccoli.
Serves 1

Method
1. Mix the garlic salt & the ground black pepper together rub onto both sides of the steak. Place onto the round tray.
2. Mix the onions with the olive oil & spread around the steak.
3. Cook on the high rack on 250°c for – **Rare 5 minutes on each side, Medium 7 minutes on each side, Well done, 10 minutes on each side.**
   This is a rough guide & will depend on the thickness of the meat.
4. Stir the onions every 3 minutes of cooking time; add the blue cheese to melt on top after the meat is cooked to your liking.
   Try with turkey fillets instead of steak, adjust time accordingly.

Stuffed Chicken Breasts
with Streaky Bacon & Sage

Ingredients
2 Chicken breasts
4 slices streaky bacon
6 mini mozzarella balls
1 tsp tomato puree
4 sprigs sage
Salt & pepper
***Serve with roast potatoes
& steamed broccoli.***
Serves 2

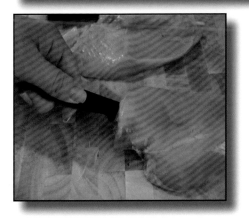

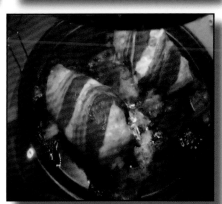

Method

1. Make a small incision with a knife at the fattest end of the chicken breast, to form a deep pocket. Repeat with the second chicken breast.
2. Stuff the pocket with half of the tomato puree & 3 mozzarella balls. Repeat with the second breast.
3. Place 2 sprigs of sage on top of each breast & wrap each with two slices of streaky bacon & season.
4. Place on the round tray & cook on the low rack at 250°c for 20 minutes turning after 10 minutes. baste the chicken with its juices using a cooks brush.
5. Turn down to 200°c & cook for a further 5 minutes.
Can change mozzarella for cheddar instead.

83

Stuffed Chicken Drum Sticks

Ingredients
8 chicken drum sticks
50g dried sage & onion stuffing mix
Boiling water
¼ tsp yeast extract
2 tsp honey
8 cocktail sticks
Garnish
Fresh lemon
Serves 4-6

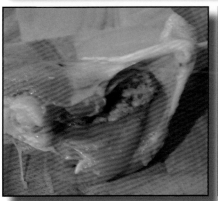
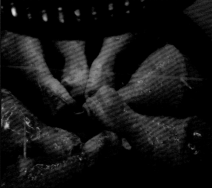

Method

1. Mix the dried stuffing mix with a little boiling water leave to soften, roll into marble size balls. Set aside.
2. Take your chicken drumstick & peel back the skin (from the thickest part) halfway down to expose the flesh.
3. With a sharp knife, make an incision into the flesh & fill with a stuffing ball.
4. Carefully roll up the skin & secure with a cocktail stick.
5. Repeat with the rest of the drumsticks.
6. Cook on the round tray on the low rack 200°c for 10 minutes.
7. Mix together the yeast extract & honey .
8. Then glaze the part cooked drumsticks & cook 12 minutes or until cooked.
    Great on a picnic.

Stuffed Courgettes

Ingredients
230g ready cooked green lentils
1½ tbsp flour   (drained weight)
1 onion (diced)
225g minced beef
4 courgettes
3 tbsp tomato ketchup
1 tbsp tomato puree
1 clove garlic (finely chopped)
1 tsp paprika
50g emmental or preferred cheese (grated)
Salt & pepper
Serve with rice & salad.
Serves 4

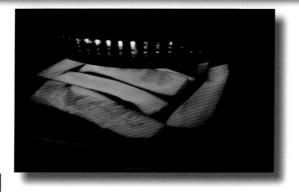

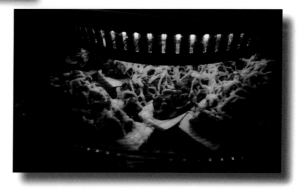

Method

1. Place the garlic, onion & minced beef in to an oven proof dish (that will fit in the halogen oven). Cook on the low rack at 250°c, stirring after 5 minutes. Continue to cook for a further 3 minutes.
2. Whilst the meat is cooking wash & dry the courgette & slice off the ends. Cut in half lengthways & scoop out the centres with a spoon.
3. Add the flour, paprika, tomato puree, tomato ketchup & green lentils to the mince & continue to cook on the low rack at 250°c for further 4 minutes. Remove & put to one side.
4. Put courgette on a round tray & put on the high rack at 250°c for 5 minutes.
5. Place the mince filling in the courgette & sprinkle with the cheese & cook on the low rack at 250°c for 10 minutes.

87

Stuffed Peppers

Ingredients
200g turkey mince
½ white onion (finely chopped)
¼ tsp paprika
¼ tsp garlic salt
1 tbsp tomato puree
2 chestnut mushrooms (finely chopped)
25g parmesan cheese (grated)
25 breadcrumbs
125g cooked rice
3 red peppers
Salt & pepper
Serve with salad.
Serves 3

Method

1. Put the turkey mince, onion, paprika, garlic salt and tomato puree In a bowl. Mix well. Transfer to the round tray and cook on the high rack at 250°c for 6 minutes, stirring after 3 minutes.
2. In a separate bowl mix the chestnut mushrooms, parmesan cheese, breadcrumbs and cooked rice. Pour in the turkey mince mixture, season well with salt and pepper. Stir.
3. Slice off the tops of the 3 peppers to make lids. Fully fill each pepper (to the brim) with the stuffing mixture and firm down well. Holding the lid in place, carefully trim a little off the base to help them stand up.
4. Place on the round tray and cook on the low rack at 150°c for 25 minutes.

Can change turkey mince for beef mince or meat substitute.

89

Turkey and Cranberry Pie with a Suet Crust

Ingredients

Filling

25g butter
500g turkey breast (diced)
1 onion (finely chopped)
5 chestnut mushrooms (sliced)
1 tsp garlic paste
1 chicken stock cube with (100ml boiled water)
1 tsp plain flour
150ml double cream
1 tbsp cranberry sauce

Suet crust

150g self-raising flour
75g suet
Salt and pepper
130ml cold water

Serves 6
Serve with roast potatoes and sweet corn or vegetables of your choice.

Method

1. Place a heatproof dish onto the low rack. Add the butter and cook at 250°c for 30 seconds, to melt. Add the turkey breast, onion, chestnut mushrooms and garlic paste. Mix thoroughly. Cook at 250°c for 15 minutes, stirring every 5 minutes.

2. Add 1 tsp plain flour & stir, Add the chicken stock and cook for a further 6 minutes, stir. Add the cream, cranberry sauce, mix & cook for 5 minutes.

3. To make the suet crust, add the self-raising flour, suet and a pinch of salt and pepper to a bowl. Slowly add the cold water (Only use amount of water needed to form a dough) Roll out the dough on a floured surface to make a crust to fit the top of the ovenproof dish.

4. Add the crust to the top of the turkey mixture, cook on the low rack at 175°c for 20 minutes then turn down to 150°c and cook for 5 minutes.
Can change turkey for chicken instead.

91

Yorkshire Puddings

Ingredients
175g plain flour
225 ml milk
85ml cold water
2 eggs
Pinch of salt
4 x 1cm cubed lard
4 ramekins (200ml size)
Serve with roast beef &
all the trimmings
Serves 4

Method
1. Place a 1cm cube of lard in the base of each heat proof ramekin dish. Put on the low rack & heat the lard for 7 minutes at 250°c.
2. Put the flour with a pinch of salt in a large bowl. Make a well in the centre. Add the eggs & start to whisk.
3. Slowly add the milk & continue whisking.
4. Add the cold water & whisk .
5. Pour the batter mixture carefully & equally, between the ramekins.
6. Cook on the low rack for 10 minutes at 250°c. Turn down to 200°c & cook for 10 minutes. Turn down to 150°c & cook for a further 5 minutes.

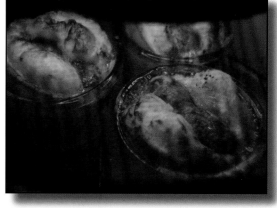

To make mini toad in the holes, add a sausage to each ramekin at stage 1, whilst heating the lard for 5 minute. Follow the rest of the recipe as method given above. See picture above.
You can make the Yorkshire pudding mixture up to 2 hours in advance and keep in fridge.

Baked Alaska

Ingredients
3 egg whites
100g caster sugar
1 large sponge flan case
5 tsp raspberry jam
5 tbsp vanilla ice cream
Serves 5

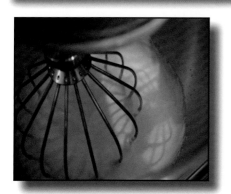

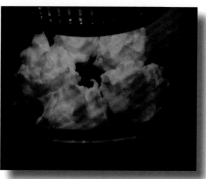

Method

1. Whisk the egg whites in a large clean, grease free bowl, until stiff peaks form. Continue to whisk, gradually adding the sugar.
2. Using a food ring or a large pastry cutter cut out 5 circles from the sponge flan case and place on the round tray. Spoon the raspberry jam equally on top of the sponges, then add a large tablespoon of ice cream on top.
3. Carefully spoon the meringue over the ice cream. Cook them on the low rack at 250°c for 4 minutes. Serve immediately.
Not to be consumed by the very young, sick or elderly as it contains semi – cooked egg.
You can make one large baked alaska instead of individual ones. 95

Chocolate Cherry Brownies

Ingredients
200g plain chocolate
155g butter (save a little for greasing
3 eggs   2 x baking parchments)
100g muscavado sugar
50g drinking chocolate powder
75g plain flour
100g glacé cherries
(soaked in 1 tbsp cherry brandy)
Baking parchment
Serve with cream or ice cream.
Serves 8

Method

1. Add a cup of boiling water to the base of the halogen oven. Break up the plain chocolate and place in a heat proof bowl. Add the butter on top. Place the bowl on the low rack at 200°c for 5 minutes. Stir to combine the chocolate & butter. Cook for a further 2 minutes then mix.

2. Line and grease a round tray with a piece of baking parchment.

3. Whisk the eggs and sugar together in a large bowl. Add the drinking chocolate powder and the melted chocolate mixture and stir. Fold in the plain flour and the cherries soaked in cherry brandy.

4. Place the brownie mixture into the prepared round tray. Leaving the boiling water in the base of the halogen oven. Cook the uncovered brownie mixture on a low rack at 160°c for 20 minutes.

5. While cooking, grease and line (with baking parchment) the steamer tray. Once the 20 minutes cooking time is up, place the lined steamer tray over the top of the part cooked brownie and turn over, keeping the brownie, sandwiched between the two round trays, place back into the halogen oven and cook for a further 15 minutes at 180°c. (to cook the base which is now facing up) See pictures. Once cooked turn back over & serve.

You can add white chocolate chips to the mix.

97

Cookie Cake

Ingredients
50g butter
50g brown sugar
1 egg
100g plain flour
½ tsp baking powder
½ tsp baking soda
1 tbsp golden syrup
1 tsp vanilla extract
100g chocolate chips
50g sultanas
Serves 6

Method

1. Cut a piece of baking parchment to fit the base of the round tray and grease well with butter.

2. Cream the butter and brown sugar together in a mixing bowl. Add the egg then sift in the flour, baking powder, baking soda and mix. Add the golden syrup and vanilla extract and mix. Fold in the chocolate chips and the sultanas.

3. Place the mixture into the greased lined round tray and place the uncovered cookie cake on the low rack and cook at 160°c for 10 minutes.

4. Meanwhile cut a piece of baking parchment to fit the steam tray and grease well with butter. After the 10 minutes cooking time, remove the cookie in its tray and to cook the base, turn over onto the second tray. Keeping the cookie sandwiched between the two trays, cook on the low rack at 180°c upside down for a further 15 minutes. Turn back over & serve.

Leave whole and can be decorated as a birthday cookie.

99

Grilled Peaches with Almond Liqueur

Ingredients
2 peaches (halved and de-stoned)
½ tsp brown sugar
1 tsp almond liquor
Garnish
Mint
Serve with thick cream.
Serves 2

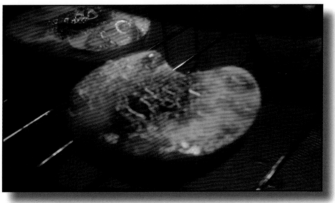

Method

1. Mix, the brown sugar and the almond liqueur together in a small bowl.
2. Place the mixture into a jug and pour equal amounts into the centre of each peach.
3. Place the peaches on the high rack and cook for 5 minutes at 250°c
   For an extra special treat serve with Chantilly cream by whisking up double cream with a dash of vanilla extract and a couple of shakes of icing sugar.

Mango and Apple Crumble

Ingredients
480g bag frozen cubed mango (or fresh)
2 cooking apples (thinly sliced)
1 tbsp brown sugar
Crumble Mix
200g plain flour
100g butter (room temperature)
100g brown sugar
25g rolled oats
¼ tsp cinnamon
Serve with custard or cream.
Serves 6

Method

1. Place the mango and apple in a heatproof oven dish, . You may need to add the tablespoon of brown sugar, depending on whether you like your fruit sweet or tart! Cook on the low rack at 200°c for 20 minutes in (total), stirring after 10 minutes then every 5 minutes.

2. Whilst the fruit is cooking, make the crumble mix by adding the plain flour, butter, 100g brown sugar, cinnamon and rolled oats into a mixing bowl. With your fingertips, combine the ingredients until it resembles breadcrumbs (or use a food processor).

3. Add the crumble to the top of the fruit and cook at 150°c for 10 minutes then turn up to 200°c for 5 minutes .
   As an alternative you can add 3 tbsp of sultanas or raisins to the fruit base.

103

Pecan Treacle Tart

Ingredients

Pastry
100g cold butter (cut into cubes)
50g caster sugar
200g plain flour
A little cold water (1 egg to glaze)
Filling
8 tbsp golden syrup
150g bread crumbs
50g pecan nuts
Zest and juice of 1 lemon
2 tbsp golden syrup (for topping)
Serve with custard.
Serves 6

Method

1. To make the pastry, put the flour, butter and
   sugar into a food processor. Blitz until it looks
   like fine bread crumbs then add cold water,
   a little at a time until a dough is formed. This
   will leave the sides of the mixing bowl clean.
2. If possible, allow to rest in the fridge wrapped
   in cling film for 15 minutes.
3. Roll out the pastry and use to line a 22cm tart dish. Prick the base
   of the pastry case with a fork. Cook on the low rack at 180°c for
   20 minutes.
4. Whilst the pastry case is cooking, mix the bread crumbs, 8 tbsp golden
   syrup, pecan nuts, lemon zest & juice in a bowl. After the cooking time,
   remove the pastry case and glaze all over with a little of the beaten
   egg. Return to the halogen oven and cook on the low rack at 220°c for
   7 minutes.
5. Add the filling to the pasty case and pour over 2 tbsp golden syrup,
   cook on the low rack at 250°c for 10-15 minutes until golden brown.
   Can be served hot with ice cream.

105

Popcorn with Toffee Sauce

Ingredients
75g popping corn
Toffee Sauce
50g brown sugar
25g butter
1 tbsp golden syrup

Serve with toffee sauce.
Serves 4

Method

1. In the base of a small heat proof bowl place the sugar, the golden syrup and the butter on top. Place this on the round tray onto the low rack in the halogen oven. Cook the sauce at 250c for 3 ½ minutes. Remove and set aside.

2. Continue to heat the round tray at 250°c for a further 3 ½ minutes.

3. With the hot sauce, with one hand use a teaspoon to keep the bowl still, whilst stirring with a fork with your other hand. Continue to stir for a full 2 minutes until the ingredients are fully mixed to form the toffee sauce.

4. Cook the popping corn on the pre heated round tray at 250°c for 8 minutes. Leave to rest in the halogen oven for 5 minutes to ensure all of the corn has popped.(a few may not pop)

5. Remove and cover with the toffee sauce
   Change the toffee sauce for salt for a savoury popcorn.

107

Raisin and Cinnamon Rolls

Ingredients

80ml warm milk
80ml warm water
25g butter
Pinch saffron (optional)
250g white bread mix (packet like you use
25g brown sugar   in a bread maker)
¼ tsp cinnamon
125g raisins or sultanas
1 beaten egg
1 tbsp apricot jam (mixed with 1 tsp of
Serves 6   boiling water to glaze)

Method

1. In a large jug, mix the warm milk, warm water, butter and saffron.
2. Place the bread mix into a large bowl slowly stirring, add the warm liquid to make a dough – (you may not need to add all the liquid), or you a food mixer. Rest for 15 minutes. Then knead again.

3. Roll out the dough onto a floured surface. Sprinkle the raisins, brown sugar and cinnamon onto the dough.
4. Carefully roll up the dough into a long sausage shape and slice into 6 circles. Grease the round pan and arrange the dough circles on top. Glaze with the beaten egg (rest in a warm place for 15 minutes).

5. Add a cup full of boiling water into the base of the halogen oven. Cook on the low rack at 200°c for 8 minutes. Turn down to 150°c and cook for a further 10 minutes or until cooked.
6. Turn out onto a plate and glaze with the apricot jam mix.
Serve warm from the oven or glaze with icing sugar mixed with lemon juice and a glacé cherry.

Books Available In Our Range

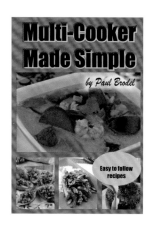

Multi-Cooker Made Simple
by Paul Brodel
Easy to follow recipes

HALOGEN COOKING MADE EASY

What's for dinner?
Meal Ideas...
Now with even more of our top tips!
Paul Brodel and Dee Hunwicks

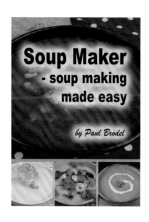

Soup Maker
- soup making made easy
by Paul Brodel

Hot Air Frying

Hot Air Frying & More
by Paul Brodel

CHOP & BLEND
BY
PAUL BRODEL

CUPCAKE CREATIONS
by Paul Brodel

Festive Feasts
by Paul Brodel

If you have any questions regarding the recipes within this book, please feel free to visit our website:

www.paulbrodel.co.uk

or email us at: **cook@paulbrodel.co.uk**